Deviled Egg Recipes

50 Recipes from America's Favorite Party Dish

Emily Benjamin

The Sharper Edge Press
Massapequa, NY

Copyright © 2011   Emily Benjamin

Printed in China

Table of Contents

The Recipes

Acknowledgements

I'm grateful to the many people who played a part in helping write and publish this book. The idea of creating a Deviled Egg Recipe Book initially seemed absurd to most – up to and including me! We all love to make and/or eat deviled eggs... but did we need a whole book about them?? But the more people I talked to about it, the more the idea seemed possible... then plausible... than somewhat necessary. I guess I learned that virtually everyone likes to eat deviled eggs, but not a lot of people know how to make them. And those that make them only seem to know of 1 or 2 ways of making them. And yet, the beauty of deviled eggs is that they can successfully be made to suit any taste – salty, spicy, or sweet; ordinary or extraordinary; light and fluffy or beefy and strong. So thank you for pushing me forward... because there were many times I thought I should have stopped.

I'd also like to acknowledge the many, many, many people who offered their recipes, tips, advice, hints, substitutions, alternatives and clever names. The creativity and ingenuity of people is astounding – even for something as "ordinary" as eggs! I thought I might have a hard time coming up with 50 or so recipes for deviled eggs. But by the time I had spoken just to friends and family, I had at least that many! The toughest part for me was to whittle down the huge list of recipes to the 50 or so that made it into this book. Even tougher was saying sorry to those people whose recipes didn't get in. Maybe we'll need a Volume 2 someday...

I'm grateful to the people who continuously cooked and tested – and judged – the various recipes we look at. I couldn't have sampled 5,000 deviled eggs by myself!

Finally, I want to thank Barbara, Mike, Chris, Lynn, and Denny... you guys put so much effort turning my scribbles into this beautiful book! And special thanks to Claudia for having the courage to run with it!

Deviled Eggs have become an American tradition. You see them at virtually every large party or family gathering. Ironically, you'll even see "Deviled" eggs at many a Church Pot Luck dinner!

Why are we so infatuated with deviled eggs? I think it's easy to see why deviled eggs have become a mainstay dish. They are relatively easy to make. They are eminently transportable. They aren't overly messy. Most recipes have been handed down the family tree, time tested for just the right mix of taste and nostalgia. And last, but certainly not least, they are downright delicious. Think about this winning formula: take a base food that virtually everyone likes (eggs), do a few simple cooking techniques to it (boiling, peeling), then add any spice, or combo of spices, that your stomach can conjure up! What's not to LOVE about deviled eggs!

Where do deviled eggs come from? The origin of deviled eggs can't be pinned down to any one specific person, date or place. The actual concept of deviled eggs begins with Ancient Rome. Spicy stuffed eggs were known in the 13th century in the area of what is now called Spain. However, the term "deviled eggs" was an 18th century invention. According to many historic cookbooks, the practice of boiling eggs, removing the yolks, combining the yolks with spices and then refilling the shells with that mixture was common by the end of the 1700's.

But what does the term "deviled" actually mean? The word "deviled" first appeared in print in the late 1700's and was used to describe highly seasoned fried or boiled dishes. By the 1800's, the term "deviled" evolved and was often used as a culinary term to describe fiery hot spiced dishes or condiments. And yes, the word was coined this way due to the symbolism of the devil and the excessive heat of his place of abode. Through the 19th century, the word deviled continued to be used to describe hot seasonings, more specifically cayenne or mustard.

In modern language, however, the word deviled has a broader meaning and is typically defined as a food that is spicy or stimulating and contains heavy seasoning. The term is "deviled" is used to describe eggs, crab, cakes, and many other dishes.

As the deviled egg "movement" has matured, people have started to look beyond grandma's secret recipe for their next deviled egg fix. We are pushing the limits, stretching the boundaries to reach tastes and textures we didn't even know existed! They have come under international influences, been built into holiday themes, and have housed exotic foods. Along they way, we've applied every conceivable point on the spicy spectrum to deviled eggs. From mild to five-alarm and back.... deviled eggs don't even take a backseat to buffalo wings in the arena of hot!

With this book, my aim was simple: give everyone a chance to see, explore, and have fun with deviled eggs. At the end of the day, that's what good comfort food is all about!

In the opening chapters, you'll learn the best methods and practices to be sure your deviled eggs come out with the right shape, flavor, color, and texture. Then, we offer up some tried and true deviled egg recipes – the recipes that cover two-thirds of all deviled egg dishes ever created. These recipes will give you a good chance to test and hone your deviled egg skills.

Then, in the later chapters, we'll explore some more exotic and unusual recipes. In "Eggs-actly What the Devil Ordered," we'll turn up the heat and find out how to really put the "deviled" in deviled eggs. Then, in "Eggs-otic and Eggs-travagant," we'll delve into deviled egg recipes that stretch the brain and the taste buds by incorporating some exotic and unusual foods in them. Lastly, we'll take a trip around the country and around the world in search of regional and international influences on deviled egg dishes.

So, without further ado: Let the deviling begin!!!

The Devil Is In The Details

How To Cook and Prep Eggs for Deviled Recipes

"It's As Easy as Boiling Water..."

 We've all heard this phrase at some point in our lives. However, when it comes to hard boiling eggs that will become your deviled masterpiece; nothing could be further from the truth! In fact, I must have come across hundreds of different "recipes", anecdotes, folk tales, family secrets, helpful hints and other tidbits about how to boil eggs when researching this book!

Well, thankfully, it's not overly complicated... but there are a few easy pitfalls awaiting you if you don't take the time and patience to follow these steps.

Before Boiling
Like many things in life, proper planning makes all the difference in how things turn out. Would you run an event without first planning it? Would you start putting an addition on your house without first buying and prepping the proper materials needed for the job? Well, maybe deviled eggs don't rate as important as those examples, but a little bit of prep will go a long way when it comes to hard boiling eggs.

Step 1: *Egg Selection*
What could be so hard about this? Nothing, really. However, if you want to make the job of peeling the eggs easier, make you sure you DO NOT use fresh eggs. You want them aged in the refrigerator for 7-10 days. Why? This brief "breather" allows the eggs time to take in air, which helps separate the membranes from the shell.

Step 2: *Centering the Yolks*
Some people out there believe that a centered yolk brings years of good fortune. So, to help center the yolks in the eggs, the night before

the eggs are to be cooked (approximately 12 hours), store your eggs on their sides in the refrigerator. Seal the egg carton with a piece of tape and turn on its side to center the yolks.

Step 3: *Use Room Temperature Eggs*
Bring your eggs to room temperature before cooking. The temperature of the egg at the start of the cooking process will affect the cooking time. An egg that is at room temperature at the start of the cooking process will require about 1 minute less cooking time than eggs taken directly from the refrigerator.

The Big Boil
This is actually the shortest and easiest part of "hard boiling" eggs. Technically, you are not hard boiling them at all. You are "hard cooking" them – in fact as you read ahead you will see that the cooking process must stop when the water boils!

Step 1: *Into the Pan*
Put the eggs in saucepan large enough to hold them in single layer. ADD cold water to cover eggs by 1 inch.

Step 2: *Heat*
HEAT over high heat just to boiling. Immediately remove the pan from the heat once it boils.

After Boiling
Just because they are cooked doesn't mean the prep work is done.

Step 1: *The Big Cover-Up*
Immediately remove the pan of eggs from the burner. COVER the pan with a tight fitting lid.

Step 2: *The Waiting Game*
LET EGGS STAND in hot water about 12 minutes for large eggs
(9 minutes for medium eggs; 15 minutes for extra large)

Step 3: *From Hot to Cold*
Then place the hot eggs under running, cold water to cool quickly. This
way of cooking is also known as "coddling." It does not toughen the
whites as boiling does. This will also help prevent discoloration of the
yolk and will also assist with the peeling process, as the cold water cre-
ates steam between the egg white and the shell which makes the shell
easier to remove.

Refrigeration is necessary for hard boiled eggs if the eggs are not to
be consumed within a few hours. Hard-cooked eggs in the shell can be
refrigerated up to one week only.

What's the Big Peel, Anyway?
Now you can start tearing the shells off…
right? Not exactly. Like everything else we've
looked at so far, peeling the eggs is another
art – and science – onto itself.   We've heard
of people rolling the eggs before peeling.
Or cracking the center with a spoon while
holding the egg up like it's about to be kicked
for a football field goal. Or blow you hot
breath on the part you are going to crack.

While I'm sure that there are all good ideas with some merit, I've settled
on what seemed to be the most consistent set of principles for peeling an
egg effectively and efficiently (and non-violently).

Step 1: Place the eggs in the pan they were cooked in and
add cold water.

Step 2: Remove the egg and gently tap the egg on a countertop. Roll it back in forth in your hand to crack it all over.

Step 3: Start peeling at the larger end, where the air pocket is, and remove the shell under running water to make the shelling easier. You must get a hold of the membrane under the shell when you remove the shell. Very fresh eggs are harder to peel. The fresher the eggs, the more the shell membranes cling tenaciously to the shells.

Slicing the Eggs

Now that the eggs have been prodded, coddled, and cajoled through the cook and peel process, its time to slice them up, remove the yolks, and start devilin'.

All but a few people use the traditional lengthwise slice. Plus, most of the existing deviled egg trays lay out this way. But for those contrarians, you can slice them vertically if you wish. There's also no magic to pulling out the yolks – just get them out without damaging the whites or making a big mess.

Now, off to the recipes...

American Favorites

What better place to start a book about Deviled Egg Recipes than with the good old fashioned recipes? These are the ones that Grandma used to make. And then Mom. And now you. And years down the road, your children and grandchildren will make them, too!

In this chapter you'll find a handful of Deviled Egg "Starter" Recipes. If I can follow them, then I think you will be able to follow them, too. These recipes fall into the "if it ain't broke, don't fix it" category.

Bring a plate of these to the office party, the backyard barbeque, or the Church supper. And rest assured, you will be bringing home an empty plate.

Beginner's Deviled Eggs

Ingredients

3 large eggs, hard-cooked

2 tablespoons mayonnaise

1/2 teaspoon prepared mustard

1 dash pepper

Directions

- Cut eggs lengthwise into halves.
- Slip out yolks and mash well with a fork.
- Mix in remaining ingredients.
- Fill whites with yolk mixture, heaping it up lightly.

Grandma's Traditional Deviled Eggs

Ingredients

6 hard-boiled eggs, peeled halved lengthwise

1/4 cup mayonnaise, low-fat okay

1 tablespoon prepared mustard

1/2 teaspoon white vinegar

1/4 teaspoon salt

1 tablespoon sugar

paprika *(to garnish)*

Directions

- Scoop egg yolks into bowl.
- Set aside egg whites.
- Add mayonnaise, mustard, vinegar, sugar, salt and pepper to yolks.
- Mash together with fork until smooth.
- Spoon mixture into egg white halves.
- Sprinkle tops with paprika.

Aunt Mae's Sweet Deviled Eggs

Ingredients

18 eggs
1 cup mayonnaise *(not salad dressing)*
1/2 cup sugar
1 tablespoon yellow mustard
paprika *(optional)*

Directions

• Boil eggs to hard-boiled stage.
• Rinse in cold water, cool and peel.
• While eggs are boiling, make sauce.
• Combine mayo, sugar and mustard and stir until smooth.
• Refrigerate, and don't be worried if sauce still has sugar crystals.
• When ready to assemble, slice eggs in half, scoop out yolks and mash.
• Take sauce out of fridge and stir again.
• Now it should be smooth.
• Mix sauce with mashed egg yolks. But don't use all at once.
• May have to add a little more until the right consistency.
• Start with 1/2 of the sauce and add more a little at a time as needed.
• Spoon into egg whites and sprinkle with paprika for garnish.

Old Fashioned Deviled Eggs

Ingredients

18 eggs
8 hard boiled eggs
1/4 cup mayonnaise *(I prefer the taste of Hellmann's)*
2 tsp heavy cream
2 tsp red wine vinegar
2 tsp dry mustard
2 tbs minced onion
1/2 tsp salt
1/ tsp sugar
black or white pepper to taste
Fresh minced chives for garnish

Directions

- Cut eggs In halve and remove yolks.
- Place yolks and all other ingredients into a food processor.
- If you are making these by hand, first push the yolks through a fine gauge sieve and then mix with other ingredients.
- Spoon or pipe mixture *(using a disposable pastry bag)* into the eggs.
- Garnish with fresh chives and store until ready for service.

Easy Deviled Eggs and Ham

Ingredients

3 hard-cooked eggs, cooled, peeled

3 slices shaved smoked ham, finely chopped

1 small kosher dill pickles, finely chopped

1 tablespoon Miracle Whip light

1 teaspoon Grey Poupon Dijon Mustard

pepper, to taste

Directions

• Cut eggs in half lengthwise.

• Remove yolks; place in bowl and mash with fork.

• Add ham, pickles, dressing, mustard and pepper; mix well.

• Spoon egg yolk mixture evenly into egg whites.

• Serve immediately or cover and refrigerate until ready to serve.

• Garnish with paprika, if desired.

Garlic Deviled Eggs

Ingredients

6 hard-cooked eggs

1/3 cup mayonnaise

1/2 teaspoon prepared mustard

2 green onions with tops, chopped

1 garlic clove, minced

1/8 teaspoon salt

Paprika

Directions

- Slice eggs in half lengthwise; remove yolks and set whites aside.
- In a small bowl, mash yolks.
- Add mayonnaise, mustard, onions, garlic and salt.
- Fill egg whites; sprinkle with paprika.
- Refrigerate until serving.

A Devil For Every Holiday

Deviled Eggs have become a mainstay of every holiday celebration. Of course Easter comes to mind as the holiday most identified with this – since there seems to be no shortage of colored eggs hiding in every corner of your refrigerator.

Most people roll out their favorite classic deviled egg dish when it comes to a holiday party or family gathering. And there's nothing wrong with that.

Some more daring, adventurous folks, however, have taken to making dishes that not only are delicious, but they also blend in visually with the holiday they are cooked for. They have become décor items as well as foods!

So please, give one of these a try on the next holiday – especially when you are looking for omething that will wow all of their senses!

Ingredients

12 eggs

1 tablespoon sweet pickle relish

1 tablespoon mayonnaise

1 pinch celery salt

1 tablespoon prepared yellow mustard

2 drops green food coloring, or as needed

1 (6 ounce) can sliced black olives, drained

Directions

- Place all of the eggs into a large pot so they can rest on the bottom in a single layer.
- Fill with just enough cold water to cover the eggs.

Continued...

- Bring to a boil, then cover, remove from the heat and let stand for about 15 minutes.
- Rinse under cold water or add some ice to the water and let the eggs cool completely.
- Peel and slice in half lengthwise.
- Remove the yolks from the eggs and place them in a bowl.
- Mix in the relish, mayonnaise, celery salt, mustard, and food coloring.
- Spoon this filling into the egg whites and place them on a serving tray. Round the top of the filling using the spoon.
- Place an olive slice on each yolk to create the center of the eye.
- Dab a tiny bit of mayonnaise in the center of the olive as a finishing touch.

Patriotic Eggs

Ingredients

3 large eggs, hard-cooked

2 tablespoons mayonnaise

1/2 teaspoon prepared mustard

1 dash pepper

Red and Blue egg dye

Vinegar

Directions

- Boil and peel eggs. After you peel your eggs make sure you run them under cold water and get every thing from the shell off.

Continued...

- Dip them till you get the color you want.
- Cut and pop the yolk out of all the WHITE eggs you plan to use and keep them separate, they will pick up die from your fingers or touching the other eggs while they're wet.
- For Red Eggs, dip eggs into 25 drops of red dye and 1/2 tsp vinegar and only 1/2 cup of water.
- For Blue Eggs, dip eggs into 20 drops of blue dye and 1/2 tsp vinegar and only 1/2 cup of water.
- Let dyed eggs thoroughly dry. Roll on a paper towel, then let them sit for a bit so the dye dries.
- Split eggs lengthwise. Remove yolks from eggs and place in a bowl.
- Mix in mayo, mustard, and pepper.
- Spoon filling back into egg whites.

Deviled Egg Easter Chicks

Ingredients

8 extra-large eggs, hard-boiled

1/2 cup heavy mayonnaise

1/8 teaspoon garlic powder

1/4 teaspoon prepared mustard (table)

1/4 teaspoon salt

1/8 teaspoon fresh coarse ground black pepper *(optional)*

4 pimento stuffed olives, slice each into 4 slices

16 slices red bell peppers, tiny triangles, can sub carrots

Directions

• Place eggs in saucepan of cold water.

• Bring to a boil over med-high heat, STIRRING GENTLY AND CONSTANTLY, *this keeps the yolks in the center.*

Continued...

- Boil and gently stir for 2 minutes.
- Place on tight fitting lid and turn off heat.
- Let sit for 25 minutes.
- Carefully put eggs into bowl of ice water. Let sit for 5-10 minutes.
- Carefully peel eggs. *This is easy if eggs are older.*
- Rinse with cold water, place on paper towel.
- Slice thin slice off bottom of each egg, *this will ensure they stand up later.*
- With paring knife, cut top third of egg off in a zig-zag pattern. CAREFULLY remove tops.
- CAREFULLY scoop out yolks. *Take your time doing this, you may need to use your paring knife to break up yolks inside to get them out.*
- Place yolks in mixing bowl, mash WELL with fork.
- Stir in rest of ingredients except olives and peppers.
- Overfill bottom egg white "shell" with filling, place top "shell" on carefully pressing very gently.
- Place on olive slices for "eyes", pressing them into the filling gently.
- Push 2 triangles of red pepper into filling to make beak.

Summer Barbeque Deviled Eggs

Ingredients

6 hard-boiled

1 tablespoon mayonnaise

3 tablespoons barbecue sauce

1 to 2 tablespoons French-fried onions

1 scallion, thinly sliced

Directions

- Boil and peel eggs. Slice eggs in half. Remove yolks.
- In a small bowl, combine egg yolks, barbecue sauce, and mayonnaise; mix well.
- Fill egg white halves with yolk mixture and place on a platter.
- Sprinkle with French-fried onions and scallions to garnish.
- Cover with plastic wrap and refrigerate until ready to serve.

Spooky Spider Deviled Eggs

Ingredients

6 hard-boiled eggs, halved

3 tablespoons mayonnaise

1/2 teaspoon ground mustard

1/8 teaspoon salt

1/8 teaspoon pepper

black olives

Directions

- Cut eggs in half lengthwise. Slip out yolks and mash.
- Stir in mayonaise, mustard, salt, and pepper.
- Cut whole olive in half.
- Put one half on mashed yolk for the spiders body.
- Thinly slice the other half for the spiders legs. Put three legs on each side.

Devilishly Good Eggs

Ingredients

6 eggs
3 tablespoons mayonnaise
1 teaspoon yellow mustard
1/8 teaspoon sugar
1/8 teaspoon salt
1/8 teaspoon ground red pepper
Roasted red peppers, for garnish
Black olives, for garnish

Directions

- Place eggs in a small saucepan and add enough water to cover them. Bring to a boil over high heat; remove pan from heat, cover, and allow to sit 20 minutes.
- Drain hot water and run cold water over eggs. Allow to cool 5 to 10 minutes before peeling.
- Slice eggs in half lengthwise and remove yolks.
- In a medium bowl, combine egg yolks, mayonnaise, mustard, sugar, salt, and ground red pepper; mix well.
- Spoon mixture back into egg whites. Decorate with roasted red peppers and olives Serve immediately, or cover lightly and chill until ready to serve.

Chips 'n' Bacon Deviled Eggs

Ingredients

6 hard-boiled eggs, halved

3 tablespoons mayonnaise

1/2 teaspoon ground mustard

1/8 teaspoon salt

1/8 teaspoon pepper

black olives

Directions

Cut eggs in half lengthwise. Slip out yolks and mash.

Stir in mayonaise, mustard, salt, and pepper.

Cut whole olive in half.

Put one half on mashed yolk for the spiders body.

Thinly slice the other half for the spiders legs.

Put three legs on each side.

Eggs-actly What the Devil Ordered

When people think about deviled eggs, most assume it will be a moderately spiced or seasoned dish. Some paprika. Some black pepper. Maybe a touch of something zestier. Something that brings otherwise bland eggs alive. In fact the definition of "deviled" is just that – any food that is spiced or seasoned heavily.

Some folks have gone to taking this to the extreme. In the same way that "buffalo" wings have come to mean any level of spiciness added to chicken wings, so, too have deviled eggs been pushed to the edge of the scalding hot abyss.

In this chapter, we will explore some of the hottest, spiciest recipes we've come across for deviled eggs. Be forewarned, however, some of these dishes or not for the faint of heart. But if you are a hot food nut, grab a glass of milk and turn up the heat with these tongue-zipping dishes.

Kickin' Horsey Eggs

Ingredients

12 hard-boiled eggs, peeled,
   halved and yolks removed to separate bowl

1/2 cup good mayonnaise

2 teaspoons yellow mustard

2 tablespoons sweet pickle relish

salt and pepper

1-2 teaspoon prepared horseradish

Directions

- Mix yolks with all other ingredients and taste to adjust seasonings.
- Use more or less of any to suit your taste.
- Sprinkle lightly with paprika.
- Chill thoroughly and serve.

Cajun Deviled Eggs

Ingredients

6 hardboiled egg

1/3 cup mayonnaise

2 teaspoons horseradish mustard

1 teaspoon cajun seasoning

Directions

- Slice the hard boiled eggs in half, carefully remove the yolks & place them in a mixing bowl.
- Mash the yolks with a fork.
- Stir in the mayo & mustard, then mix until creamy.
- Add the Cajun seasoning & blend well.
- Spoon the mixture back into the hollows in the egg whites.

Jalapeno Bacon Deviled Eggs

Ingredients

8 eggs, hard boiled and peeled

1/2 teaspoon mustard powder

1/4 teaspoon sugar

1/2 tablespoon white vinegar

1 dash garlic powder

1/3 cup mayonnaise *(not Miracle Whip, it has sugar)*

salt or celery salt

3 -4 tablespoons minced onions

2 -5 tablespoons minced pickled jalapeno peppers

4 slices crispy bacon, chopped fine

1 quart ziploc bags *(for piping the yolk mixture into the egg)*

paprika *(to garnish, chives or cilantro leaves would
    be good, too)*

Continued...

Directions

- Cook your eggs and bacon at the same time if you don't have leftovers.
- Slice the eggs lengthwise in half and pop the yolks into a small mixing bowl.
- Mash the yolks thoroughly with the next four ingredients.
- Add the mayo in 3rds till it's the consistency you like, mashing any lumps of yolk. I use all the mayo but some people don't want to consume that much. More mayo makes a lighter filling.
- Salt to taste, then add the onion, jalapeno and bacon and mix well.
- Place in the quart ziploc bag *(fold the top edge well down so you don't get yolk all over it and spoon the mixture into one of the corners.)* Unfold the bag top, smooth out any air, twirl the bag to seal the egg into it and clip the corner off the bag.
- Pipe the yolk into the egg halves. It makes quite a bit so you can mound the yolk over on the solid white part of the egg, as you fill it.
- Garnish.

Devilishly Deviled Eggs

Ingredients

6 hard-boiled eggs

2 green onions, minced fine

1/2 small kosher dill pickles, minced fine

1 tablespoon finely minced parsley

1 tablespoon mayonnaise

1 tablespoon cream cheese, room temp

1 1/2 teaspoons french's yellow mustard

1/2 teaspoon sugar

1/2 teaspoon ground cumin

1/2 teaspoon pepper

1/4 teaspoon seasoning salt

Tabasco sauce

1 pinch garlic powder

2 pinches onion powder

paprika, to garnish

minced chives, to garnish

black caviar, to garnish

Continued...

Directions

- Peel & halve hard boiled eggs.
- Put yolks into a bowl, mash & mix well with mayonnaise, mustard, cream cheese, sugar, cumin, pepper, garlic powder, onion powder, green onion & pickles.
- Taste mixture before adding seasoning salt. You may need less than 1/4 teaspoon. Season to taste with seasoning salt & tabasco.
- Stuff egg white halves with yolk mixture. You can do this with a spoon, or you can put the yolk mixture into a quart-size plastic bag & snip off one corner to act as a pastry bag. Or if you want to get really fancy you can use an actual pastry bag with a fancy cake decorating tip on the end.
- Squeeze yolk mixture into egg white halves. Refrigerate before serving to allow yolk mixture to set. Don't garnish until just before you are ready to serve *(especially if you are using paprika)*.

Spicy Sweet Football Eggs

Ingredients

1 dozen hard-cooked eggs, peeled

1/2 cup mayonnaise

3 tablespoons mango chutney

1/8 teaspoon ground red pepper

Kosher salt to taste

Garnish: sliced fresh chives

Directions

- Cut eggs in half lengthwise; carefully remove yolks.
- Mash yolks;
- Stir in mayonnaise, chutney, and red pepper until blended.
- Spoon yolk mixture evenly into egg white halves.
- Sprinkle evenly with desired amount of salt.
- Garnish, if desired. Chill until ready to serve.

Zippy Deviled Eggs

Ingredients

12 hard-cooked eggs

1/4 cup mayonnaise

3 tablespoons chili sauce

1 teaspoon prepared mustard

1/4 teaspoon hot pepper sauce

Paprika

Directions

- Slice eggs in half lengthwise.
- Remove yolks and set whites aside.
- In a small bowl, mash yolks.
- Stir in the mayonnaise, chili sauce, mustard and hot pepper sauce.
- Pipe or stuff into egg whites.
- Sprinkle with paprika.
- Refrigerate until serving.

Salsa Mexicana Deviled Eggs

Ingredients

12 large hard-boiled eggs

1 cup finely grated cheddar cheese

1/4 cup salad dressing *(use Miracle whip salad dressing or similar, not mayo for this)*

2 teaspoons Miracle Whip, mustard mania *(optional but good to use)* or 1 -2 teaspoon prepared mustard *(optional but good to use)*

1/4 cup medium salsa *(or use mild)*

1 tablespoon sour cream

2 -3 large green onions, finely chopped

1/4 teaspoon garlic powder

seasoned salt and pepper

finely grated cheddar cheese *(any amount desired for topping)*

paprika *(optional)*

Continued...

Directions

- Drain the salsa over a fine strainer. *(push the liquid through the strainer with a spoon to speed up the process)*
- Set aside.
- Using a sharp knife slice the hard-boiled eggs in half.
- Carefully remove the yolks from 12 eggs and place into a food processor
- Place the 24 egg whites halves on a plate or serving platter.
- Add in all remaining ingredients except finely shredded cheddar cheese, seasoned salt and pepper; process for about 10 seconds or until smooth.
- Add in seasoned salt and pepper to taste, and process again.
- Transfer the mixture to a bowl.
- Add in 1 cup finely grated cheddar cheese and mix with a spoon until blended.

Ingredients

1/4 cup chopped cooked chicken *(store cooked rotisserie chicken for me)*

buffalo wing sauce to cover chicken, plus 5 teaspoons

6 hard-boiled eggs, peeled cut in half and yolks mashed in a bowl

1/4 cup softened butter

1/4 teaspoon Tabasco sauce

1 teaspoon chopped celery, plus extra to garnish

Continued...

Directions

- Cover chicken with enough Buffalo sauce; let sit at least 5 minutes.
- Combine yolk and butter.
- Stir in celery and Tabasco.
- Add chicken and 5 teaspoons of Buffalo sauce.
- Place mixture in zip lock bag with the corner cut off *(big enough to squeeze out mixture)*.
- Fill egg whites with mixture and garnish with celery.
- Enjoy right away or let it sit at room temperature for 15-20 minutes for flavors to develop.

Chipotle Deviled Eggs

Ingredients

12 large eggs

1/3 cup plus 2 tablespoons mayonnaise

2 to 3 teaspoons finely chopped canned chipotle chiles

24 fresh cilantro leaves

Directions

- Place eggs in large saucepan. Add enough cold water to cover. Bring to simmer over high heat. Reduce heat to low; simmer gently 5 minutes.

- Remove from heat, cover, and let stand 10 minutes.

- Drain eggs; cover with ice and water and let stand until cold.

Continued...

- Peel eggs and cut in half lengthwise.
- Spoon yolks into small bowl; arrange whites on platter.
- Finely grate yolks on small holes of box grater into medium bowl.
- Mix in mayonnaise, then 2 teaspoons chopped chipotle chiles. Add more chopped chiles, if desired, for more heat.
- Season filling to taste with salt, if desired.
- Using pastry bag fitted with 1/2-inch-diameter star tip, pipe filling into egg whites.
- Cover and chill eggs at least 2 hours and up to 1 day.
- Press 1 cilantro leaf into filling in each egg and serve.

Eggs-otic and Eggs-travagant

Most deviled egg dishes use eggs and some condiments and spices. But nowadays, people have incorporated virtually every imaginable food into their favorite develied egg recipe. From shellfish to salmon, from nuts to mushrooms to assorted other foods, people are pulling in the exotic more and more extravagant foods into deviled eggs. In the process, they are creating wild new flavors, extraordinary new textures, and quite simply, incredible new dishes. In addition, exotic spices are being added, and combined with other spices to create multi-dimensional tastes.

This chapter samples some of these more exotic recipes. If you like the foods or spices being used, you should give them a try. Or, better yet, throw in your own personal favorite exotic food and create something new!

Shrimp Deviled Eggs

Ingredients

6 hard-boiled eggs

1 lb shrimp, peeled and
   cooked *(reserve 12 for garnish, chop the rest)*

1 medium cucumbers, peeled and diced

1 teaspoon ketchup

1 teaspoon lemon mayonnaise *(add 1/2 teaspoon of
   fresh lemon to mayonnaise stir)*

1 green onions, sliced thin

1 teaspoon salt • 1/4 teaspoon pepper

Directions

- Carefully slice hard boiled eggs in half.
- Cut and drain cucumber, by letting cucumber sit in a
  colander for about 5 minutes.
- Mix all ingredients with egg yolks together, *(except reserved
  shrimp and fresh herbs)* gently. Spoon back into empty hard
  boiled egg shell.
- Gently place the reserved shrimp on top of the egg yolk
  mixture, adding a small sprig of fresh herb.
- Serve with a little toast point or cracker.

Crabby Deviled Eggs

Ingredients

12 hard-cooked eggs

1 (6 ounce) can crabmeat

- drained, fluked and cartilage removed

1/4 cup mayonnaise or salad dressing

2 tablespoons sweet pickle relish

1 tablespoon prepared mustard

2 teaspoons seafood seasoning

1/4 teaspoon pepper

Directions

- Slice eggs in half lengthwise. Remove yolks and set the whites aside.
- In a small bowl, mash yolks with a fork.
- Add crab, mayonnaise, relish, mustard, seafood seasoning and pepper; mix well.
- Stuff or pipe into egg whites.
- Refrigerate until serving.

Ingredients

12 eggs

4 tablespoons white sugar

1/4 teaspoon salt

1/4 teaspoon onion powder

1/8 teaspoon garlic powder

1/8 teaspoon white pepper

2 tablespoons yellow mustard

1 tablespoon mayonnaise

1 tablespoon creamy salad dressing

1 tablespoon cider vinegar

paprika for garnish *(optional)*

Continued...

Directions

- Place the eggs in a saucepan in a single layer with enough water to cover by 1 inch. Cover the saucepan and bring the water to a boil over high heat. Once the water is boiling, remove from the heat and let the eggs stand in the hot water for 15 minutes.
- Pour out the hot water, then cool the eggs under cold running water. Peel once cold.
- Dry the eggs thoroughly with paper towels, and slice them in half lengthwise.
- Remove the yolks, and place in a bowl.
- Mash the yolks with a fork, and stir in the sugar, salt, onion powder, garlic powder, and white pepper.
- Add the mustard, mayonnaise, salad dressing, and vinegar, one at a time, stirring to incorporate each ingredient before adding the next.
- Mound a heaping teaspoonful of the yolk mixture into the cavity of each egg half, and sprinkle with paprika.

Pecan Stuffed Deviled Eggs

Ingredients

6 eggs, hard-boiled & peeled

1/2 cup mayonnaise

1 teaspoon onions, grated

1/2 teaspoon fresh parsley, chopped

1/2 teaspoon dry mustard

1/8 teaspoon salt

1/3 cup pecans, coarsely chopped

Directions

- Cut eggs in half lengthwise and carefully remove yolks.
- Mash yolks in a small bowl; stir in mayonnaise, onion, parsley, mustard, and salt. Blend well.
- Stir in pecans.
- Spoon or pipe yolk mixture evenly into egg-white halves.
- Garnish, if desired *(paprika, fresh parsley, etc)*.

Truffled Deviled Eggs

Ingredients

12 eggs, hard-boiled & peeled

6 tablespoons mayonnaise

2 teaspoons Dijon mustard

2 teaspoons black truffle oil

1/3 cup Black Truffles, thinly sliced

2 teaspoons lemon juice

2 teaspoons finely chopped chives

Salt and pepper

Directions

- Hard-boil 12 eggs, cool, peel, halve, and carefully remove the yolks; reserve the whites.

- Combine egg yolks, 6 tablespoons mayonnaise, 2 teaspoons Dijon mustard, 2 teaspoons black truffle oil, 2 teaspoons freshly squeezed lemon juice, and 2 teaspoons finely chopped fresh chives in a medium nonreactive bowl. Season well with salt and freshly ground black pepper and mix well until yolks are broken up and ingredients are evenly incorporated.

- Evenly pipe or spoon yolk mixture into reserved egg white halves. As desired, top with thinly sliced black truffle

Ingredients

6 large eggs

3 tablespoons minced smoked salmon *(about 1 oz.)*

3 tablespoons minced green onions

3 tablespoons softened cream cheese

1 tablespoon sour cream

1 teaspoon Dijon mustard

2 teaspoons lemon juice

1/4 teaspoon salt

1/8 teaspoon ground red pepper

Garnishes:

   fresh dill, smoked salmon slivers, sweet paprika

Continued...

Directions

- Place eggs and enough water to cover in a saucepan over medium heat; bring to a boil.
- Cover, remove from heat, and let stand 15 minutes.
- Drain; return eggs to saucepan, and add enough cold water and ice to cover.
- Let cool. Remove shells from eggs, halve each egg lengthwise, and scrape yolks into a bowl. Reserve egg whites.
- Combine yolks, salmon, and next 7 ingredients, mashing with a fork until well blended.
- Spoon filling into reserved whites, cover loosely with plastic wrap, and refrigerate up to 2 days.
- Garnish, if desired.

Wasabi Deviled Eggs

Ingredients

12 large eggs *(hard-boiled, cooled & halved)*

6 tablespoons Mayo

2 teaspoons Chinese Mustard

4 teaspoons Wasabi paste

2 tablespoons lime juice

2 tablespoons chopped nori

Salt and pepper

Optional Roe, Salmon, eel or favorite sushi food

Directions

• Hard-boil 12 eggs, cool, peel, halve, and carefully remove the yolks; reserve the whites.

Continued...

- Combine egg yolks, 6 tablespoons mayonnaise, 2 teaspoons Chinese mustard, 4 teaspoons wasabi paste, 2 teaspoons freshly squeezed lime juice, and 2 teaspoons chopped nori in a medium nonreactive bowl. Season well with salt and freshly ground black pepper and mix well until yolks are broken up and ingredients are evenly incorporated.
- Evenly pipe or spoon yolk mixture into reserved egg white halves. As desired, top with deep-fried nori strips and uni (sea urchin), salmon, or tuna roe, or unagi (eel), or crab.

Loaded Deviled Eggs

Ingredients

12 **large eggs** *(hard-boiled, cooled & halved)*

6 **slices bacon** *(cooked crisp & crumbled)*

2 teaspoons fresh chives

2 teaspoons white vinegar

2 tablespoons finely shredded mild cheddar cheese

1/4 cup sour cream or 1/4 cup buttermilk

paprika

Directions

- Transfer egg yolks from halves to mixing bowl & combine with remaining ingredients.
- Add the sour cream or buttermilk last & use more as needed to reach desired smoothness.
- Spoon yolk mixture into halves. The bulk will have grown substantially, so pile it high & "dust" with a sprinkle of paprik

Angelic Deviled Eggs

Ingredients

6 eggs

¼ cup low-fat cottage cheese

3 tablespoons prepared fat-free ranch dressing

2 tablespoons Dijon mustard

2 tablespoons minced fresh chives or dill

1 tablespoon diced well-drained pimento or raosted peppers

Directions

- Slice eggs lengthwise in half. Remove yolks, reserving 3 yolk halves. Discard remaining yolks or reserve for another use.
- Place egg whites, cut sides up, on serving plate; cover with plastic wrap.
- Refrigerate while preparing filling.
- Combine cottage cheese, dressing, mustard and reserved yolk halves in food processor; process until smooth. (Or, place in small bowl and mash with fork until well blended.)
- Transfer cheese mixture to small bowl; stir in chives and pimiento.
- Spoon into egg whites.
- Cover and chill at least 1 hour.

Guacamole Stuffed Deviled Eggs

Ingredients

6 hard-boiled eggs *(cold, halved and yolks removed)*

1 avocados, mashed

2 tablespoons salsa, your favorite

Garnish: 12 cilantro leaves

Directions

- Slice eggs lengthwise and remove yolks.
- Mix avocado with salsa. Note that the avocado is a substitute for the egg yolks
- Place a scoop into each half.
- Top with a cilantro or parsley and serve.

Deviled Eggs with Capers and Tarragon

Ingredients

6 hard-boiled eggs

1 tablespoon mayonnaise

2 tablespoons extra-virgin olive oil

1 1/2 teaspoons Dijon mustard

2 tablespoons minced celery

4 teaspoons chopped fresh tarragon

1 tablespoon minced drained capers

2 teaspoons minced shallot

Sliced celery

Directions

- Shell eggs, then cut in half lengthwise. Transfer yolks to small bowl and mash with fork.
- Mix in oil, mayonnaise, and mustard.
- Stir in minced celery, tarragon, capers, and shallot.
- Season to taste with salt and pepper.
- Spoon yolk mixture into whites.
- Garnish each with celery slice.
- Can be made 4 hours ahead. Cover loosely and refrigerate.

A Devilish World of Eggs

Deviled Egg Recipes From Across The Country – And Around The Globe!

They call America "the melting pot" for good reason. Not only are we made up of people from all corners of the world, but every aspect of our culture has been influenced by people and customs from around the globe. Our foods are no different. Some of our country's most treasured dishes and delicacies are imported, borrowed, and founded in the foods and recipes from other counties.

It seems quintessentially American, therefore, that we take a tried and true American favorite – Deviled Eggs – and traverse the country and the globe to find new and inspiring ways that prepare and flavor our favorite dish.

The "Devilish World of Eggs" chapter explores some of the tastiest, most exotic, and sometimes unbelievable deviled eggs recipes that either come from or are inspired by tastes and flavors from around the globe.

Spicy Southwestern Deviled Eggs

Ingredients

12 hard-cooked eggs, peeled

1/2 cup mayonnaise *(not Miracle Whip)*

1 1/2 teaspoons ground mustard

1/2 teaspoon seasoning salt

1/2 teaspoon ground cumin

1/2 teaspoon chili powder

1/4 teaspoon cayenne pepper

chives *(optional)* or green onions, chopped *(optional)*

1 dash paprika *(to garnish)* *(optional)*

Continued...

Directions

- After hard boiling, peel eggs and rinse them to be certain there are no little bits of shell adhering, dry them with a paper towel, then slice them in half lengthwise.
- Pluck out the yolks, putting them in a small bowl; setting the whites aside on a serving plate.
- Mash the yolks with a fork or masher.
- Stir in mayonnaise, dry mustard, cumin, chili powder and cayenne until smooth and creamy.
- Spoon or pipe yolk mixture into egg halves. Sprinkle lightly with paprika and garnish with chives or chopped green onion, if desired.
- Cover with plastic wrap and refrigerate until ready to serve. Makes 12 *(2 halves servings)*.

Russian Style Deviled Eggs

Ingredients

1 lb chicken livers

20 large eggs

10 mushrooms

1 onion

Mayonnaise to taste

Salt & pepper to taste

Paprika

Directions

- Boil chicken livers *(they will take about 15-20 minutes)* until tender.
- While they're cooking, boil eggs until hard-boiled, about 15 minutes.

Continued...

- Peel and cut eggs in half, reserve the white halves and yolks separately.
- Chop and saute onions and mushrooms *(salt to taste)* and set aside.
- When gizzards are done, put them through a food processor until they're finely chopped *(you're trying to get a pate consistency)*.
- When finished, add yolks to the meat and mash until well mixed.
- Put the mushroom and onion mixture through the food processor and add to the rest of the filling, mixing until smooth.
- Add mayonnaise to taste - the resulting filling should be creamy but not overly greasy - and add salt and pepper to taste.
- When filling is finished, replace it into the egg white halves with a teaspoon.
- Arrange decoratively on a plate and sprinkle with paprika for decoration

Southern Style Beet Pickled Deviled Eggs

Ingredients

1 dozen eggs, hard boiled and peeled

1 cup apple cider vinegar

15 ounces sliced beets, from a can

1/2 cup brown sugar

1 tablespoon peppercorns

1 teaspoon kosher salt

sliced raw onions, to taste

1/2 cup mayonnaise

2 teaspoons Dijon mustard

1 tablespoon butter

1/8 teaspoon white pepper

1/8 teaspoon Old Bay Seasoning

basil, fresh, chopped

Continued...

Directions

- Drain beets and reserve juice. Set beets aside.
- Combine vinegar, beet juice, brown sugar, peppercorns, and salt in a sauce pan and boil until sugar is dissolved. Remove from heat and cool.
- Layer eggs, beets, and onion in a jar large enough to fit *(with room for the brine)*, and fill the jar with the cooled brine.
- Soak eggs for at least 16 hours, up to 20 *(suggested: 17 hours,)*.
- After brining, remove the eggs and cut in half. Scoop out the yolks into a medium-large bowl.
- Remove a few slices of onion from the jar, and finely chop/mince *(if desired)*.
- With a stand or hand mixer, whip together the egg yolks, mayo, butter, onion, and seasonings, make sure to taste and adjust seasoning to preference. Mix in minced onion, if using.
- Pipe the yolk mixture into the pinked whites.
- Top with chopped fresh basil,.

Mediterranean Deviled Eggs

Ingredients

12 hard-cooked eggs,
  peeled and cut in half lengthwise

1/3 cup mayonnaise

1/4 cup hummus

1/4 cup chopped black olives

1 teaspoon lemon juice

1/8 teaspoon salt

1/8 teaspoon black pepper

1 tablespoon chopped fresh parsley

Directions

- Boil Eggs. Peel. Slice eggs in half and remove yolks.
- In a medium bowl, combine egg yolks, mayonnaise, hummus, black olives, lemon juice, salt, and black pepper; mix well.
- Fill egg white halves with yolk mixture and place on a platter. Sprinkle each egg with chopped parsley. Cover with plastic wrap and refrigerate until ready to serve.

Thai Red Curry Deviled Eggs

Ingredients

6 eggs Hard-Cooked Peeled Eggs

2 tablespoons mayonnaise

2 tablespoons Thai Red Curry Sauce

1 teaspoon lime juice

1 scallion, chopped, plus extra for garnish

1/4 teaspoon kosher salt

Directions

- Cut each hard-cooked egg in half lengthwise.
- Scoop the egg yolks out into a small bowl.
- Add the mayonnaise, curry sauce, lime juice, scallions, and salt to the bowl with the yolks. Mash together until combined.
- Fill the yolk mixture into the egg white halves and garnish with a few chopped scallions.

Italian Style Deviled Eggs

Ingredients

6 eggs

1/4 cup mayonnaise

1 -2 tablespoon spicy brown mustard

1 tablespoon Italian salad dressing mix

1 tablespoon parmesan cheese

1/2 teaspoon pepper

sliced black olives *(optional)*

paprika *(optional)*

Directions

• Boil, cool and peel eggs.

Continued...

- Cut eggs in half lengthwise, carefully scoop out yolks and place them in a small bowl.
- Mash egg yolks with a fork.
- Add mayonnaise, Italian dressing mix, mustard, Parmesan cheese and pepper. Blend well.
- Scoop or pipe yolk mixture into egg halves.
- Garnish with black olive slices and paprika if desired.
- Refrigerate until ready to serve.

Caribbean Deviled Eggs

Ingredients

6 eggs

1 tablespoon mayonnaise

1 dash hot pepper sauce

1/4 teaspoon pepper

1 tablespoon butter

1 tablespoon salt

1 tablespoon onion juice

4 stuffed olives, sliced

Directions

- Place eggs in a sauce pan and cover with cold water.
- Bring to a boil and cook for ten minutes.

Continued...

- Remove from heat and discard hot water. Allow cold water from tap to run over eggs until cool.
- Remove shell and cut eggs in half.
- Remove yolks to a small bowl.
- Mash with a fork and then add mayonnaise, pepper sauce, pepper, butter, onion juice, and salt. Mixture should be the consistency of a thick paste.
- Using a pastry bag or spoon fill the egg whites with the egg yolk mixture.
- Chill for a couple of hours.
- Serve garnished with olive slices or parsley.

Ingredients

12 large eggs

1/2 cup mayonnaise

2 teaspoons Dijon mustard

2 teaspoons sweet pickle juice

1 teaspoon Worcestershire sauce

1/2 teaspoon salt

1/4 teaspoon paprika

1/8 teaspoon cayenne pepper

Continued...

Directions

- Cook eggs in simmering water for 20 minutes, cool under running water.
- Peel and cut eggs in half lenghtwise, remove yolks and set whites aside.
- Put still warm yolks into a plastic food storage bag with mayonnaise, mustard, pickle juice, worcestershire sauce and seasonings; squeeze bag to mash yolks and mix ingredients.
- Refrigerate filling and eggs whites seperately. Fill egg whites just before service.
- Sprinkle eggs with paprika before service.

Ingredients

6 eggs

1 cup Greek yogurt or 1 cup regular yogurt

2 tablespoons sun-dried tomatoes, finely chopped

1 teaspoon smoked paprika

1/4 teaspoon salt

1 shallots, thinly sliced

1/4 cup oil

Directions

- If using regular yogurt, line a strainer with a coffee filter, place over a bowl or cup, and place yogurt in

Continued...

the filter. Let drain for 4 hours or overnight. Discard the water and use the remaining yogurt in the recipe.

- Place eggs in a pot and cover with cold water so that it covers the eggs by 1 inch. Heat on stove until boiling.
- Remove from heat and cover with lid. Set timer to 15 minutes.
- After 15 minutes, immediately drain eggs and run under cold water or immerse in a Ice bath. Peel eggs.
- Slice eggs in half and scoop out yolks into a small bowl. Set the whites aside.
- Smash the yolks with the back of a fork. Add 1/2 cup yogurt and mix well. Continue to add 1 tbsp of yogurt until desired consistency is reached.
- Mix in sun-dried tomatoes, salt, and paprika.
- Heat oil in a skillet over medium-heat. When oil is hot, test with a shallot; when the shallot instantly sizzles it is ready. Cook shallots in oil until browned. Drain on paper towels and salt lightly while still hot.

Indian Deviled Eggs

Ingredients

6 hard-boiled eggs

3 1/2 tablespoons mayonnaise

3 tablespoons minced green onions

1 tablespoon minced seeded jalapeno chiles *(or to taste)*

1 1/2 teaspoons minced mango chutney

1/2 teaspoon scant garam masala

finely chopped radishes, to garnish

Directions

- Shell eggs, then cut in half lengthwise.
- Transfer yolks to small bowl and mash with fork.
  Mix in mayonnaise. Stir in next 4 ingredients.
  Season with salt and pepper.
- Spoon yolk mixture into whites. Top generously with
  chopped radishes.

Asian Deviled Eggs

Ingredients

12 hard-cooked eggs, peeled and cut in half lengthwise

1/3 cup mayonnaise

1 teaspoon sesame oil

2 tablespoons toasted sesame seeds *(with 2 teaspoons reserved)*

1 teaspoon wasabi powder

1/8 teaspoon salt

1/8 teaspoon black pepper

1 to 2 scallions *(green onions)*, sliced

Directions

- Boil and Shell eggs, then cut in half lengthwise.
- Remove egg yolks, transfer to a small bowl and mash yolks with a fork.
- In a medium bowl, combine egg yolks, mayonnaise, sesame oil, and sesame seeds *(excluding the reserved 2 teaspoons)*, wasabi powder, salt and black pepper; mix well.
- Fill egg white halves with yolk mixture *(see Tip)* and place on a platter. Top each egg with sliced scallion and sprinkle with reserved sesame seeds. Cover with plastic wrap and refrigerate until ready to serve.

Greek Deviled Eggs

Ingredients

6 eggs

1 cup Greek yogurt or 1 cup regular yogurt

2 tablespoons sun-dried tomatoes, finely chopped

1 teaspoon smoked paprika

1/4 teaspoon salt

1 shallots, thinly sliced

1/4 cup oil

Directions

• If using regular yogurt, line a strainer with a coffee filter, place over a bowl or cup, and place yogurt in the filter. Let drain for 4 hours or overnight. Discard the water and use the remaining yogurt in the recipe.

- Place eggs in a pot and cover with cold water so that it covers the eggs by 1 inch. Heat on stove until boiling. Remove from heat and cover with lid. Set timer to 15 minutes.
- After 15 minutes, immediately drain eggs and run under cold water or immerse in a ice bath. Peel eggs.
- Slice eggs in half and scoop out yolks into a small bowl. Set the whites aside.
- Smash the yolks with the back of a fork. Add 1/2 cup yogurt and mix well. Continue to add 1 tbsp of yogurt until desired consistency is reached.
- Mix in sun-dried tomatoes, salt, and paprika.
- Heat oil in a skillet over medium-heat. When oil is hot, test with a shallot; when the shallot instantly sizzles it is ready. Cook shallots in oil until browned. Drain on paper towels and salt lightly while still hot.
- Using a small spoon, fill each egg half with the yolk mixture. Top each egg with one or two shallot slices immediately before serving.

Notes & Ideas:

Notes & Ideas:

Notes & Ideas:

Notes & Ideas: